Learn How to Play the Fingerstyle Way

ASAP

Christmas
FOR
GUITAR

By James Douglas Esmond

ISBN 978-1-57424-272-0
SAN 683-8022

Cover by James Creative Group

Copyright © 2011 CENTERSTREAM Publishing, LLC
P.O. Box 17878 - Anaheim Hills, CA 92817

www.centerstream-usa.com

About this Book

For this book I have chosen from three genres: 1) The well known sacred hymns which are a regular part of most Christmas services, i.e. "Joy To The World" and "O Come All Ye Faithful," 2) The popular favorites which have become a standard on the radio at Christmas-time, i.e. "Jolly Old St. Nicholas" and "Here We Come A-Wassailing," and 3) several less known and beautiful Christmas carols from other parts of the world, some originally made famous on the guitar. Both "The Son of Mary" and "Villancico De Navidad" are examples of this; the first of which was written by Miguel Llobet, the famous guitarist, teacher and transcriber and the latter by Agustin Barrios Mangiore, the great Paraguayan guitar virtuoso. Both of these composers and pieces served as my main inspiration for writing this book, as they both demonstrate the beauty that this instrument can display and the very essence of the Christmas spirit in music.

Table of Contents
and CD Track List

Foreword

Guitar music has always had a special place during the Christmas season. For instance there is the famous story of Silent Night being written originally for guitar due to the organ being broken. I believe that the celebration of the infant Jesus lends itself well to this intimate instrument. Even pieces that are usually bolder and louder take on different character when arranged on this for it. I have chosen some less known but beautiful pieces from around the world as well as classic Christmas hymns like "Joy To The World."

This book is organized progressively and is constituted of pieces that are developmental in nature for a beginner's technique. It is therefore recommended but not necessary to go through the book in a step-wise fashion.

I hope you enjoy the pieces and find them to be helpful on your journey as a guitarist as well as find these arrangements to be fun and practical. Merry Christmas!

Biography
James Douglas Esmond

James Douglas Esmond started playing the guitar in his teens. He received his Bachelor's of Music Theory and Classical Guitar performance from Ithaca College, Ithaca, N.Y. Upon graduating he became involved in church music. He has held positions in various churches, as a guitarist, organist, singer and conductor. In addition to his church work, he also teaches Guitar and Piano at Blue Sky Studios in Delmar, N.Y., and writes and arranges compositions in various genres and styles. He currently serves as the Organist/Music Coordinator at Newtonville Methodist Church in Loudonville, N.Y. He resides in Albany N.Y. with his wife Meighan and daughter Evelyn. You can visit him on the web at : jdesmondmusic.com.

Playing Tips

1. Good King Wenceslas
This piece presents an easy introduction to the most basic finger patterns used in this book.

2. The Holly And The Ivy
Keep the left hand very light and flexible in this piece. This will help with the articulations, etc.

3. He Is Born
The beginning of this piece is a simple A chord and therefore the placement of this chord to start the piece, even
though not all notes are immediately used, will be very helpful. Look for other places in the piece that are similar.

4. The Son Of Mary
Use this as a reinforcing piece for the notes that are higher first position reading by saying notes out loud while
playing. Use index and middle for the top line. Work this line separately for awhile before adding the bass line.

5. Still, Still, Still
The bass line to this piece goes low and there are also lower voiced chords which will require a bit more attention.

6. Jolly Old St. Nicholas
Practice the melody by itself a lot to get a very good, even sound. Make sure to de-emphasize the middle voices.

7. O Come All Ye Faithful
The left hand in this piece can be worked on it by "blocking" (practice moving from chord to chord) the left hand and practicing the motions that the left hand uses. Also practice the bass line and right hand motions alone.

8. Here We Come A Wassailing
Practice the shifts in this piece very carefully and slowly. Be careful to keep the thumb of the right hand close.

9. Joy To The World
Practice this piece in a similar way to the last. Practice the melody and bass line separately as well.

10. Villancico De Navidad
Practice the melody and bass line separately at first. Pay close attention to the places where you can use the 2nd string for melody instead of shifting on the 1st.

11. Carol Of The Bells
Get familiar with the repeating middle line so it can be put into the background while the top voice can be focused on more.

12. O Holy Night
Practice the Melody a lot by itself, being careful to shape it and work on having a good volume and even tone. Look for the places where chord changes are easy to see and work on those by blocking them.

Good King Wenceslas

arr. by J.Douglas Esmond

The Holly and the Ivy

arr. by J.Douglas Esmond

He is Born

Traditional French
arr. by J.Douglas Esmond

Triumphant
♩=140

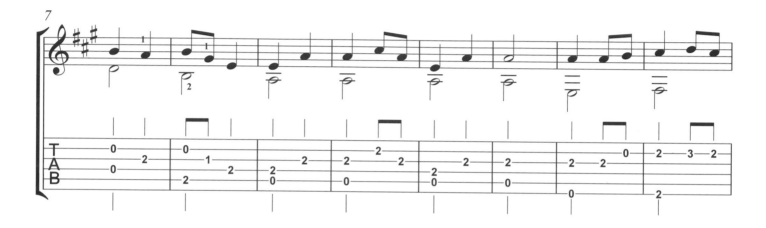

Fine

D.C. al Fine

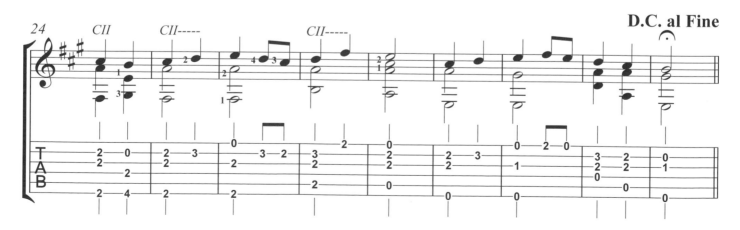

The Son of Mary

Traditional Catalan
arr. by J. Douglas Esmond

Gently rocking

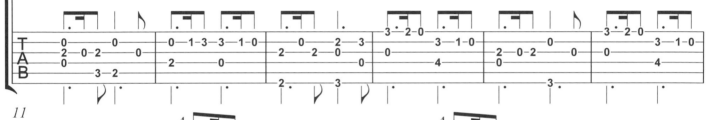

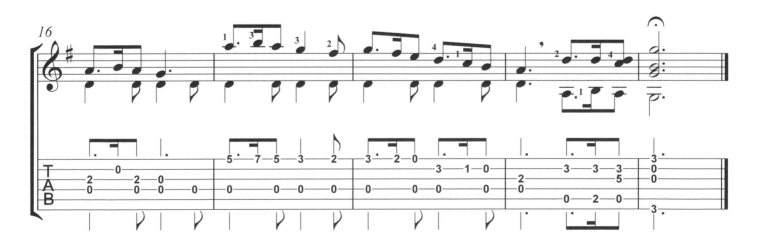

Still, still, still

Soothingly
♩=88

Traditional German,
arr. by J.Douglas Esmond

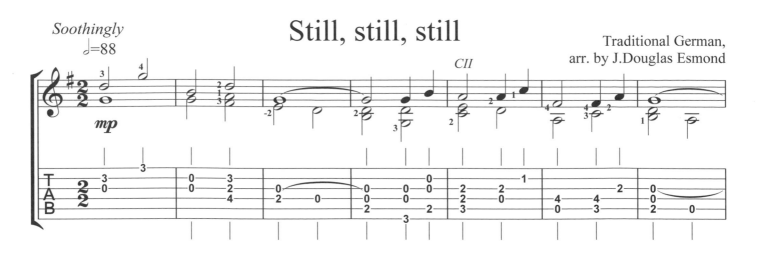

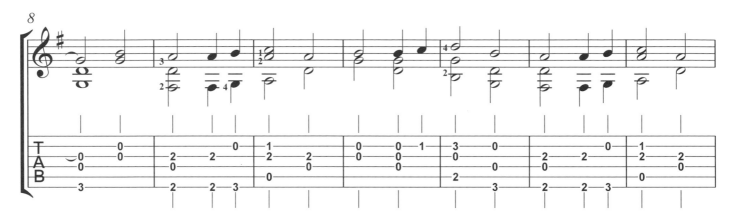

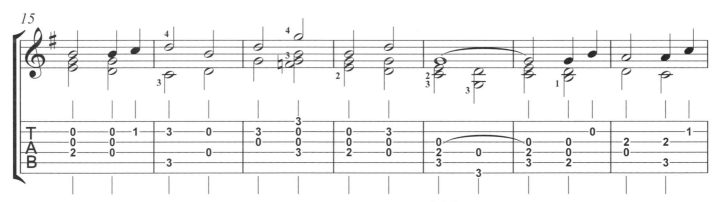

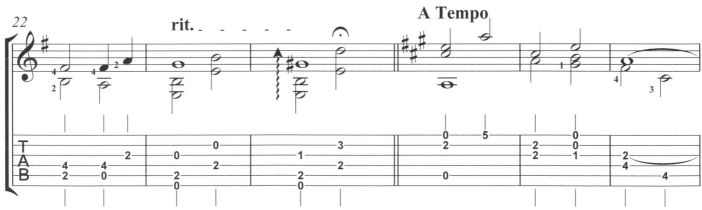

HOW LONG TO KEEP THE CHRISTMAS TREE: A VISUAL GUIDE

Jolly Old St. Nicholas

arr. by J.Douglas Esmond

O Come all ye faithful

HOW TO MAKE A CROOKED CHRISTMAS TREE LOOK STRAIGHT

Here we come a Wassailing

arr. by J.Douglas Esmond

Joy to the World

G.F.Handel
arr. by J.Douglas Esmond

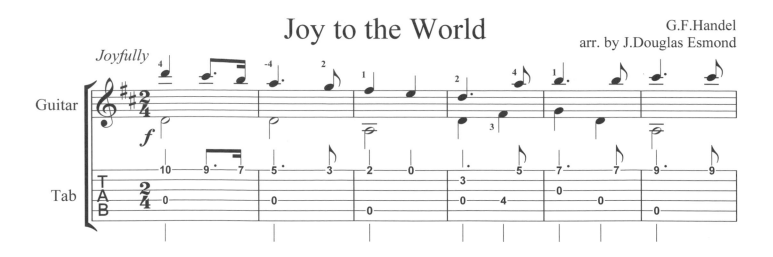

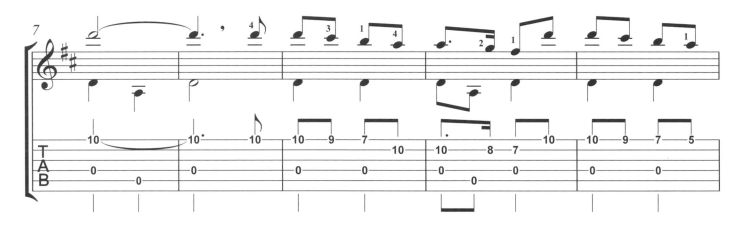

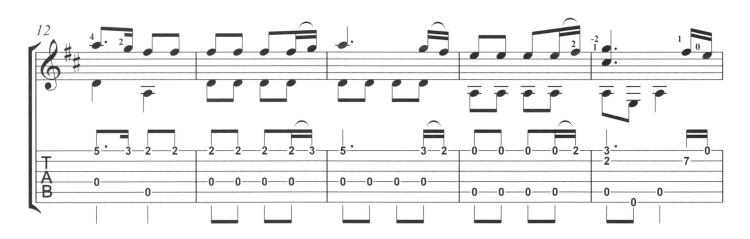

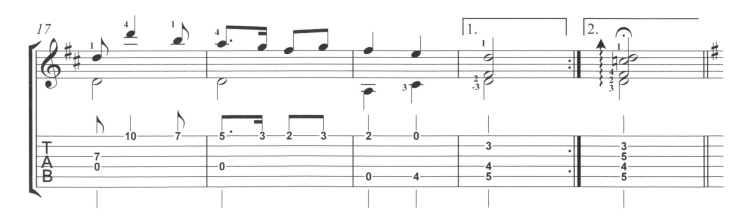

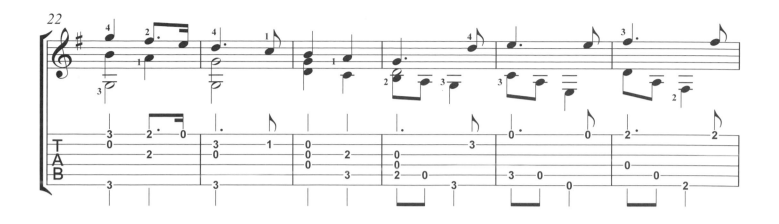

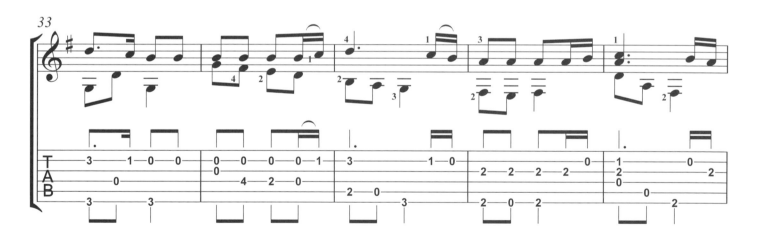

rit. _ _ _ _ _ _ _ _ _ _ _

Villancico de Navidad
(Christmas Carol)

Augustin Barrios
arr. by J.Douglas Esmond

Peacefully

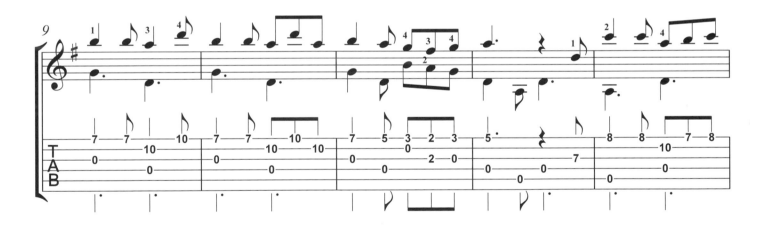

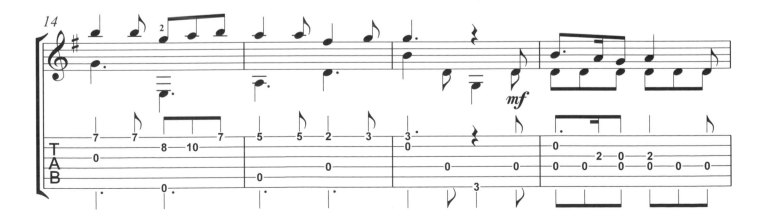

Carol of the Bells

Trance-like, mysterious

Traditional Ukrainian
arr. by J.Douglas Esmond

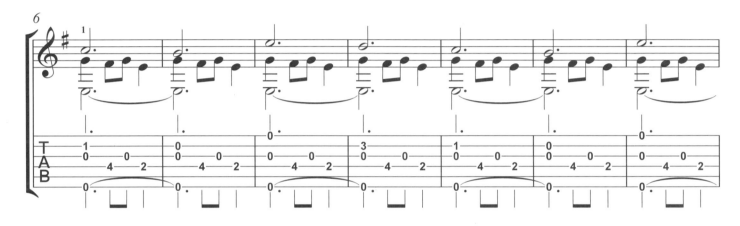

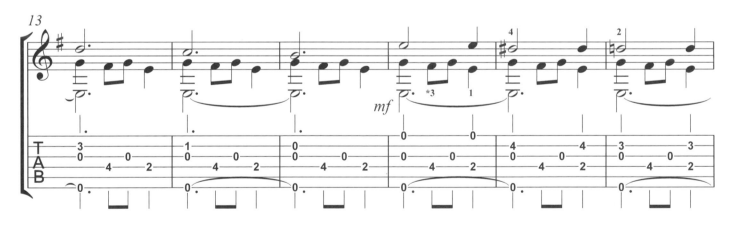

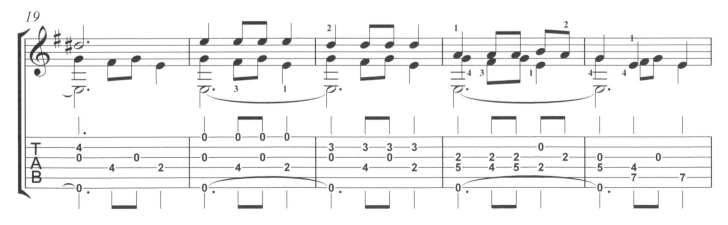

O Holy Night

Reverently
♩.=54

arr. by J.Douglas Esmond

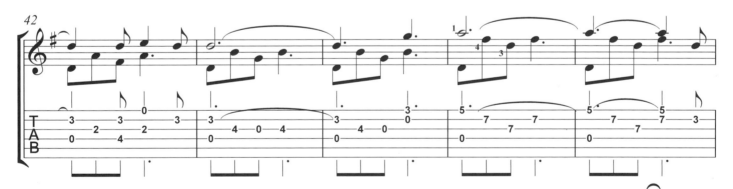

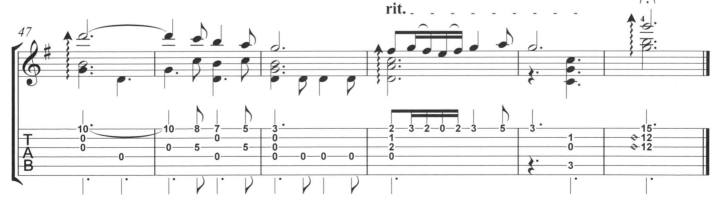

More Great Christmas Books from Centerstream...

CHRISTMAS SOUTH OF THE BORDER
featuring the Red Hot Jalapeños
with special guest
The Cactus Brothers
Add heat to your holiday with these ten salsa-flavored arrangements of time-honored Christmas carols. With the accompanying CD, you can play your guitar along with The Cactus Brothers on: Jingle Bells • Deck the Halls • Silent Night • Joy to the World • What Child Is This? • and more. ¡Feliz Navidad!

00000319 Book/CD Pack $19.95

A CLASSICAL CHRISTMAS
by Ron Middlebrook
This book/CD pack features easy to advanced play-along arrangements of 23 top holiday tunes for classical/fingerstyle guitar. Includes: Birthday of a King • God Rest Ye, Merry Gentlemen • Good Christian Men, Rejoice • Jingle Bells • Joy to the World • O Holy Night • O Sanctissima • What Child Is This? (Greensleeves) • and more. The CD features a demo track for each song.

00000271 Book/CD Pack $15.95

CHRISTMAS UKULELE, HAWAIIAN STYLE
Play your favorite Christmas songs Hawaiian style with expert uke player Chika Nagata. This book/CD pack includes 12 songs, each played 3 times: the first and third time with the melody, the second time without the melody so you can play or sing along with the rhythm-only track. Songs include: Mele Kalikimaka (Merry Christmas to You) • We Wish You a Merry Christmas • Jingle Bells (with Hawaiian lyrics) • Angels We Have Heard on High • Away in a Manger • Deck the Halls • Hark! The Herald Angels Sing • Joy to the World • O Come, All Ye Faithful • Silent Night • Up on the Housetop • We Three Kings.

00000472 Book/CD Pack $19.95

JAZZ GUITAR CHRISTMAS
by George Ports
Features fun and challenging arrangements of 13 Christmas favorites. Each song is arranged in both easy and intermediate chord melody style. Songs include: All Through the Night • Angels from the Realm of Glory • Away in a Manger • The Boar's Head Carol • The Coventry Carol • Deck the Hall • Jolly Old St. Nicholas • and more.

00000240 .... $9.95

CHRISTMAS SOUTH OF THE BORDER
featuring The Cactus Brothers
with Special Guest
Señor Randall Ames
Add heat to your holiday with these Salsa-flavored piano arrangements of time-honored Christmas carols. Play along with the arrangements of Señor Randall Ames on Silent Night, Carol of the Bells, We Three Kings, Away in a Manger, O Come O Come Immanuel, and more. Feliz Navidad!

00000343 Book/CD Pack $19.95
00000345 Book/CD Pack $19.95

DOBRO CHRISTMAS
arranged by Stephen F. Toth
Well, it's Christmas time again, and you, your family and friends want to hear some of those favorite Christmas songs on your glistening (like the "trees") Dobro with its bell-like (as in "jingle") tone. This book contains, in tablature format, 2 versions of 20 classic Christmas songs plus a bonus "Auld Lang Syne" for your playing and listening pleasure. The arrangements were created to make them easy to learn, play, remember, or sight read. So get playing and get merry!

00000218 .... $9.95

CHRISTMAS MUSIC COMPANION FACT BOOK
by Dale V. Nobbman
For 50 beloved traditional tunes, readers will learn the story of how the song came to be, the author and the historical setting, then be able to play a great arrangement of the song! Songs examined include: Away in a Manger • Deck the Halls • Jingle Bells • Joy to the World • O Christmas Tree • O Holy Night • Silver Bells • We Wish You a Merry Christmas • What Child Is This? • and more!

00000272 112 pages $12.95

THE ULTIMATE CHRISTMAS MUSIC COMPANION FACT BOOK
by Dale Nobbman
This book provides comprehensive biographical sketches of the men and women who wrote, composed, and translated the most famous traditional Christmas songs of all time. Their true-life stories and achievements are fascinating and inspirational for anyone wanting to know more about the people behind the music. 144 pages.

00001178 .... $24.95

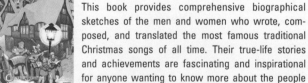

P.O. Box 17878 - Anaheim Hills, CA 92817
(714) 779-9390   www.centerstream-usa.com